THE
JOHN RYAN
ECCLESIASTICAL
FUN BOOK

MAYHEW-McCRIMMON
Great Wakering

First published in Great Britain in 1973 by

MAYHEW-McCRIMMON LTD
10-12 High Street
Great Wakering Essex

ISBN 0-85597-078-2

Printed and bound by Tindal Press Ltd
Chelmsford Essex

John Ryan writes

Because I am by trade a humourist, albeit largely for children, I thought when I was asked to compile this anthology that it would be an easy enough thing to do. Certainly it was easy to begin with. I wrote a letter appealing for contributions to all the newspapers and though the 'nationals' with the exception of the *Daily Mirror* were unable to find space, the religious press was more helpful and printed my letter. The *Jewish Voice* of Southend quoted me their advertising rates. Within a few weeks I had received over a thousand funny stories and set about choosing a hundred or two. And there the problems began.

If anyone can actually read all the anecdotes in this book at a sitting, they will begin to know what I mean. After the first hundred or so the stoutest sense of humour begins to wilt. There are, for example, the tales of the innocent utterances of children in church. I have heard plenty within my own family and know how charming they sound to  fond parents and how tedious to others. There are the anecdotes which sound so amusing when spoken and fall so flat on the printed page. There are the improper stories, often wildly funny but liable to offend more sensitive readers. I hope I have drawn the line with reasonable discretion.

Some jokes are so hoary that I have included them only out of respect for old age. And some are so new that I suspect they may have been repeated from television programmes which I do not happen to have seen. For any such plagiarisms I plead ignorance and apologise to the originators.

 The compilation of a book like this has in itself had its lighter moments. There was for example the matter of the retired bishop who wrote to my publishers submitting a manuscript of a devotional nature for possible publication. Unfortunately it became mixed with the humorous material which was rapidly accumulating in their office and the standard letter of acknowledgement was dispatched to the bishop as follows: "Thank you for writing to me with your suggestions for the John Ryan Ecclesiastical Fun Book. If I can use your material I will certainly do so." With or without the good bishop's contribution I hope this collection will justify the hopes of everyone who buys it.

A kindly Bishop went up to a little girl struggling to reach the door-bell. "Shall I ring it for you?" he asked. The child nodded, and the Bishop obliged. The angelic little face turned up to him, and said: "Now run like Hell!"

A Rev James Saint once lived in Brighton. One of his letters went astray and was delivered to Bridlington. It was returned to sender, marked by the Post Office: "No saints in Bridlington, try Brighton."

In answer to an advertisement for an organist and choirmaster, lady or gentleman: "I have been both for several years."

A clergyman and his wife, long childless, had adopted a baby, and all the parish were talking about it. At a meeting of the parish ladies, two spinsters were overheard giving their approval. Said one: "I think it's simply splendid, and such a modest way to have a baby."

The Minister delivered a short address at the infant dedication service. "Think," he said, "think of the future of this dear child. One day he may become a minister like myself, or perhaps a gallant airman or a sea-captain. He may even become Prime Minister. What is this child's name?"
    The father replied: "Mary Jane."

God said to Abraham: "Come forth."
He came fifth and was disqualified.

"It's stopped raining."

Curate: "Are you suggesting, Vicar, that I put more fire into my sermons?"

Vicar: "No, I am really trying to suggest that you put more of your sermons into the fire."

A pious Catholic bought a parrot. When he brought it home the good man was horrified to hear the parrot say: "Hiya boys — my name's Mimi . . . I'm a bad girl. Come upstairs and have some fun!" At this moment, the parish priest arrived, and to the parishioner's horror, the bird repeated the same words.

Noting the man's dismay, the Priest said: "Don't worry, bring the bird round to the presbytery. I have two good Catholic birds there who do nothing but recite the Rosary together. They will surely bring your sinful parrot back to God."

The parrot was duly brought to the Priest's house and there sure enough were two parrots in a cage reciting the Rosary. The wicked parrot was set down beside them and to begin with the other birds took no notice. Then the new arrival cocked its head on one side and said: "Hiya boys — my name's Mimi . . . I'm a bad girl. Come upstairs and have some fun!"

"Throw your beads away, George," said one of the presbytery birds to the other. "Our prayers are answered."

"But don't worry — we'll respect the minority denominations . . ."

"What is your reason for not attending church?" asked the Vicar.

"To tell you the truth," said the parishioner, "the reason is that one finds so many hypocrites there."

'"Don't let that keep you away," said the jovial padre, "there's always room for one more."

A bishop was driving his car carelessly and got involved in an accident. He pretended to sympathise with the other driver and made him drink some whisky to steady his nerves. "Aren't you having some too?" asked the other driver.

"No thanks," replied the bishop, "I'm going to call the police now."

The Pope was approached by the superintendent of the Vatican swimming bath and asked whether he would allow mixed bathing. The reply was favourable: "Yes, on Friday mornings." The Pope happened to be strolling near the swimming bath the next Friday and was astonished to see some scantily-clad females in the pool. He summoned the superintendent and asked: "What does this mean?"

"Well, your holiness, you said that we could have mixed bathing," came the reply.

"Oh, I didn't mean that sort; I meant Catholics and Protestants."

Jones: "I don't think the new Rector is up to the old one."

Brown: "Neither do I. He takes twenty minutes to put me to sleep, and the old one used to do it in ten."

In our churches there is often a lack of spiritual fruit, but there are always plenty of religious nuts!

When Bishop Wand was enthroned in Saint Paul's Cathedral, he had to follow tradition and bang on the door with his crozier before he was admitted. There was some delay in opening the door. "Do you think we've come to the right place?" asked the Bishop of his chaplain.

An Anglican Priest is reported to have said: "Of course I believe in the Apostolic Succession—how else could I believe that my bishop is in direct line of succession from Judas Iscariot?"

A certain Bishop had a chaplain who used to accompany him on his travels. The chaplain was much embarrassed when at a Confirmation Service the Bishop asked the children the question: "Why do I so often travel round the Diocese with a crook?", and received the answer from a small girl: "Because you are trying to convert him."

The Bishop had heard of a good opening for an address. The speaker had begun: "I hope my wife will forgive me when I say that some of the happiest years of my life were spent in the arms of another woman."

The ladies sat up. The speaker added: ". . . she was my mother." Smiles all round.

At the next opportunity the Bishop tried it out. He got as far as "in the arms of another woman". There was an uneasy silence, and then the Bishop added: "and I can't for the life of me remember who she was."

A vicar was leaving his parish to take up a new appointment, and went round to say goodbye to his parishioners. One of them said: "Oh Vicar, we old women will miss you most of all. We always feel you are one of us."

We are the sweet selected few,
The rest of you are damned.
There's room enough in Hell for you;
We can't have heaven crammed."

(from a hymn sung years ago by a sect in Hyde Park)

From the minutes of a Parochial Church Council: "Since the former secretary had left the area and the former minutes could not be found, it was moved, seconded, and carried that the minutes of the last meeting be adopted as they would have been read had they been found."

When the Archbishop of York was attending a dinner, the toastmaster leaned over him and whispered in his ear: "Speak well into the microphone, Sir, the agnostics here are terrible."

A Rabbi and a Catholic priest were talking together. "Tell me," said the priest, "strictly under the seal of the confessional and all that, have you ever indulged in a bit of tasty roast pork?"

"Well, I must admit, I did, just once," said the Rabbi.

"And, Father, what about you—you're supposed to be celibate—whisper in my ear—have you ever had a woman?"

The priest hesitated and then nodded shamefaced.

The Rabbi slapped him on the back "It's a lot nicer than pork, isn't it?" he laughed.

Religion from the Aerosol,
Is quite a new conceit,
To save the Church from verbiage,
Entirely obsolete;
When faith and hope and charity,
Are mixed with perfumes gay
And all the Vicar needs to do
Is murmur, "Let us spray."

Those incense-burning thuribles
Are very nearly dead;
So methods technological
Are utilized instead,
Creating thus an atmosphere,
To aid the simple prayer,
With modern thurif-aerosols,
That sanctify the air.

The aerosol of Penitence,
Has yet to be fulfilled;
But essences of Happiness
Are readily distilled;
The scent of Generosity
Has also found a spray,
At festivals of Stewardship
And even Easter Day!

For meetings ecumenical
The aerosol is fine,
Diffusing clouds of fellowship
And brotherhood divine;
Though, sometimes one may criticize
The emotional intent,
Complaining that the sentiment
Was not the scent he meant.

So now we learn to vaporize
The antidotes of Sin,
By pressurized diffusion
From a neat and handy tin;
Thus Charity is aerosoled,
To each and every man,
And, sweetly odoriferous,
We practise what we can.

S. J. Forrest

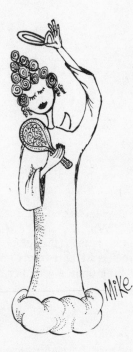

A child had the misfortune to swallow a half-penny. His mother cried: "Run for the Doctor."

But his father said: "No, run for the Parson, he can get money out of anybody."

A Cardinal was sitting next to a Rabbi at a public luncheon. "When," enquired the Cardinal of the Rabbi, "may I have the pleasure of offering you a slice of this excellent ham?" Back came the reply: "At your Eminence's wedding!"

The following is part of a notice in English displayed outside a convent hospital in Spain: "The sisters harbour all diseases and are indifferent to religion."

A poor old nun arrived at the Pearly Gates, and was admitted without any fuss or bother, told where to go, and her name ticked off on the list. The next arrival was a Cardinal, and for him a red carpet was laid out, a squad of angels played a trumpet fanfare, and Gabriel came personally to meet him.

A man who had been watching found this difficult to understand. He asked Saint Peter: "Why was so much fuss made of the Cardinal, when surely the nun had led a much harder life and deserved more notice than she got?"

Saint Peter replied: "My dear chap, nuns are two-a-penny up here, we get dozens every week, but we've not had a Cardinal for over a hundred years."

A Catholic priest, an Anglican parson, and a Rabbi were discussing what they did with the collections from their services.

The Catholic said he put all his on the table, and drew a straight line down the middle, giving one half to God and keeping the rest for himself. The Anglican said he also put all his collection on the table, but drew a squiggly line, giving one side to God and the other to himself. The rabbi said he did neither of these things, but threw all his up in the air, and whatever God caught He could keep, and whatever He missed, he kept for himself!

"Churchyard maintenance is becoming increasingly difficult, and it will be appreciated if parishioners will cut the grass round their own graves."

(from a church magazine)

The Bishop came to stay at a convent school to preside over the taking of final vows by some of the nuns. A small boarding pupil wrote home next week: "It has been very interesting here. The Bishop came to stay for the weekend, and now all the sisters have become Mothers."

A Christian lady told a congregation: "Once I was a withered branch, but now I am a blooming Christian."

Earnestly she went on to the subject of personal evangelism and added: "From that time I became a fisher of men, and have been fishing for men for the last ten years."

A Monk had a very knowing donkey, who would stop and start at very simple commands. After much heart searching, the monk eventually parted with it to a fellow friar.

The seller gave the buyer explicit instructions, saying: "When you want the animal to stop, say 'Amen,' and he'll stop, and when you want him to go, say, very clearly, 'Praise the Lord'."

The donkey changed hands, and the friar went merrily on his way, finding that the donkey responded perfectly to his instructions. As they travelled along the cliff-top pass, the friar momentarily forgot the stopping word until they reached the very edge of the cliff, then remembering, shouted "Amen" and the animal stopped dead.

The friar leaned over the animal's head and saw the rugged rocks hundreds of feet below, and with relief, he sighed "Praise the Lord!"

A Jew was asked: "Why are you all so clever and intelligent?"

"It is a dear secret," he replied.

"I am prepared to pay," continued the inquirer.

£50 exchanged hands.

"You see," said the Jew, "we eat a lot of fish, and if you eat this fish head it will do the trick for you."

The buyer started munching the fish head and suddenly remarked: "A whole fish costs 70p and you charge me £50 for a fish head."

"You see, now you are beginning to become intelligent," replied the Jew.

At a banquet the Apostolic Nuncio to France (Mgr Roncalli, later Pope John XXIII) found himself seated next to an elegant lady in a dress cut over-generously low in the neck. When dessert was served, he invited her to take the apple which he held out to her. Since the lady showed surprise at this gesture, Mgr Roncalli added: "Do take it, Madam, please do. It was only after Eve ate the apple that she became aware of how little she had on."

(Lady Priscilla Collins)

"I'd agree provided, of course, that it was linked to increased productivity."

"I have some exciting news for you all," said Reverend Mother. "We have been designated an experimental Convent. I don't know the full details but in general principle we are going to become a Mixed Community and in future we will be known as Nunks."

Two schoolmasters who were formerly colleagues met in the other world.

"What a wonderful place Heaven is after those schools we taught in," said one.

"My friend, this is not Heaven," replied the other.

"My boy," said the boss, "do you believe in life after death?"

"Yes, sir."

"Then that makes everything just fine," the boss went on tenderly.

"About an hour after you left yesterday to attend your grandfather's funeral, he came to see you."

When I was Bishop of Leeds I celebrated the Silver Jubilee of my priesthood. The unfortunate children were told to write an essay on "Our Bishop". One small boy wrote an essay of which the final sentence was: "Another thing about our bishop is that he has been a pest for twenty-five years."

(Cardinal Heenan)

A nun stopped a man on his way into a pub and remonstrated with him on the evils of drinking. "Alcohol isn't as bad as all that," he said, "you really ought to try a drop."

After some argument the nun agreed. "I can't go in," she said, "but if you bring me out a double gin in a tea-cup, I'll try it."

The man went in and ordered a double gin in a tea-cup. "God Almighty!" said the publican. "Not that bloody nun again!"

A dear old parson was preaching in a Cambridge College chapel to a congregation of men undergraduates. His theme was the parable of the Wise and the Foolish Virgins. Leaning over the pulpit, he said, earnestly: "Ah! My dear, young friends, I wonder what you would have done—watched with the wise, or slept with the foolish."

The following is an account made out by a Belgian painter, who had been employed renovating an old church.

	£	s	d
Corrected the Ten Commandments ...	1	10	0
Embellished Pontius Pilate and put a new ribbon in his bonnet		8	8
Re-plumed and gilded right wing of the Guardian Angel		15	0
Put a new tail in the rooster of Saint Peter and mended his comb		12	0
Washed the servant of the High Priest and put carmine on his cheek ...		1	0
Renewed Heaven, adjusted two stars, and cleaned the moon	1	16	0
Re-animated the flame of Purgatory and restored souls	6	6	0
Revised the flames of Hell, put a new tail on the Devil, mended his left hoof, and did several jobs on the damned	1	16	6
Rebordered the robe of Herod and re-adjusted his wig		17	3
Put new spotted dashes on the son of Tobias, and dressing on his sack ...		7	6
Cleaned the ear of Balaam's ass and shod him		9	0
Put earrings in the ears of Sarah ...		9	2
Put a new stone in David's sling ...		1	8
Decorated Noah's Ark	1	4	0
Mended the shirt of the Prodigal son and washed his neck	7	10	0

A very pompous bishop, who was well known to be under his wife's thumb, once asked a class of Sunday School children: "Who is it that sees all, knows all, and before whom even I am a mere worm?"

To his horror the palace page-boy replied: "Please, sir, the missus."

When William Doane was Bishop of Albany, New York, he adopted the usage of English Bishops by signing his name with that of his See. One day he called on the Rector of Buffalo and left a card, on which he had written "William Albany." Not to be outdone, the Rector, whose name was also William, returned the call, leaving his card bearing the inscription "Buffalo Bill."

The preacher's discourse was dry and long and the congregation gradually melted away. The sexton tiptoed up to the pulpit and slipped a note under one corner of the Bible. It read: "When you are through, will you please turn off the lights, lock the door and put the key under the mat?"

A lady sitting next to a famous and witty bishop at dinner observed in the course of conversation: "My Aunt was prevented at the last moment from sailing in the ship which foundered last week. Would you not call that the intervention of providence?"

"I can't tell," replied the bishop, "I do not know your aunt."

As Pat lay on his death-bed, the priest said to him: "Pat, you've given a lot of trouble in your life, but I know that you're a decent man at heart. Now that you are dying, will you not accept God and renounce the Devil?"

Pat thought for a moment and then replied: "Father, I'm quite ready to accept God . . . but right now I don't feel I'm in a position to antagonise anybody!"

A theological student named Fiddle
Refused to accept his degree.
"It is bad enough to be Fiddle,"
He said, "Without being Fiddle, D.D."

Years ago two clergymen completed their quarter
century as Rector and Curate. They were so un-
popular that the congregation failed to mark the
occasion, so they dined together. One rose to pro-
pose the toast of the partnership. "Sit down," said
the other. "You know that together we have emptied
the church."

"That's my reason for the toast," replied the first.
"Had we not been together we should have emptied
two churches."

The following notice is said to be in a church in
Devonshire: "If you must put buttons in the collection, please do not tear them off the hassocks."

The eight year olds went to confession for the first
time. Suddenly the priest heard a whisper.

"Charles, Charles, lend me some sins."

The answer came promptly: "Don't be silly, I've
only got three myself."

A Benedictine monk and a Jesuit were both very heavy smokers to the extent that their consciences were troubled. Both consulted their superiors. The Benedictine told his abbot that he smoked while he read his office, and was told that this was very wrong. The Jesuit merely asked his superior whether there was any harm in praying while he smoked . . . and was praised for his piety.

A small child came out of church looking thoughtful, and said to her parents: "I don't think that was fair, one man did all the work, and another one took all the money."

In a parish church, a Sunday school teacher was telling her class about the various important parts of the building — the altar, the font, and so on. Then she asked: "Do you know what the north chapel is called?"

One small boy, hesitantly: "The Lady chapel."

Teacher: "That's right. And what is the south chapel called?"

Chorus of small boys: "The gents."

Sign seen on a church notice board in Nottingham: "Come inside and have your faith lifted."

A Scots preacher was enlarging vividly on the pains of Hell, for which, he inferred too many of his congregation were quickly heading. "Aye," he said, "wheen ye find yersels in the fiery-furnace because ye didna heed the word o' the Lord, ye'll be crying oot: 'O Lord we didna ken. We didna ken!' An the Lord in his infinite maircy, will sternly answer: 'Aweel, ye ken the noo'!"

A certain Bishop complained of the size of his Palace. "Why," said he, "it's got forty bedrooms."

His hearer replied: "And only thirty-nine articles to put in 'em."

One day a Quaker farmer was milking by hand a troublesome cow called Blossom. When the pail was almost full, Blossom kicked it over, spilling all the milk. The farmer gritted his teeth and started all over again, whereupon Blossom repeated the performance.

The farmer took the cow firmly by the horns and hissed: "Thee knows, Blossom, I am a Quaker and therefore cannot beat thee. Thee knows, Blossom, I am a Quaker and therefore I cannot swear at thee. But what thee doesn't know, Blossom, is that to-morrow I'm selling thee to a Baptist, and then God help thee!"

"We *did* consider re-transmitting the very first programme — 'til it was pointed out that maybe nobody
would notice the difference . . ."

When her young son arrived home from Sunday School his mother noticed he was eating a bar of chocolate. She asked him where he had got the money from to buy it.

"Oh, the 5p you gave me this morning," he replied.

"I gave you that for Sunday School."

"I know . . . but the Vicar let me in free."

The cassocked deacon was strolling through the park when a black maxi-coated girl approached him. As she drew level with him she said quietly: "Snap."

A Jew was asked: "Why is it you Jews invariably answer a question by another question?"

"Why not?" came the prompt reply.

When the Bishop of Chester said that Christmas stamps should have a religious message on them, Punch Magazine suggested that "Lord deliver us" would be very suitable.

On an aeroplane, a Roman Catholic priest was sitting next to a Free Church Minister. The hostess came along with a tray of drinks, and asked the priest if he would like a sherry. He thanked her, and took one.

She asked the minister if he too would like a sherry. "Madam," he replied, "I would rather commit adultery."

At this the priest said: "Well, if there's a choice, I'll have the same as him."

There was an old priest of Dun Laoghaire*
Who stood on his head for the Kaoghaire
    When his people asked why
    He explained it all by
The latest liturgical thaoghaire.

*Pronounced "Dun Leary" (a town in Ireland)

The vicar of a small village owned a rather decrepit bicycle. He was often to be seen riding it around the village. The village policeman longed to catch the vicar committing a traffic offence, but had not succeeded. In desperation, he decided to wait at the traffic lights at the bottom of a steep hill, so that when the vicar approached, he could turn the lights to red, and the vicar would be unable to stop.

The next day, he carried out his plan but to his astonishment, the vicar managed to stop just in time. The same thing happened each day for a week, and the policeman gave up in disgust. He went over to the vicar and asked him how he did it.

"Ah, my friend," replied the vicar, "God is always with me."

"I've got you now. Two on a bicycle!" said the policeman.

A little girl, whose church did not have a choir, was taken by her mother to a neighbouring church where there was a surpliced choir. She whispered in dismay to her mother: "They're not *all* going to preach, are they?"

The laundry-man called at the monastery to ask if they had any dirty habits.

The American newspaper the *Saint Louis Review* published an article on the stresses and strains of the Catholic Church in England. Alongside they ran a picture of Cardinal Heenan playing the violin.

The specialist tailors, in secret researches,
Derived from the study of numberless churches,
Impart to these collars mysterious fluids
Obtained from the potions and herbs of the Druids.

Insidious liquors, by force esoteric,
Develop a serious mien in the cleric,
Restraining the wearer, by powerful laces,
From any desire to kick over the traces.

So long as his collar retains its connection,
Your parson is safe from surrounding infection;
Intact in a ring of secure insulation,
From every invasion of wordly temptation.

But, once he discards his symbolical collar
He leaps from his gloom and emotional squalor;
Reveals himself ready for orgy and revel,
And even admits he's a bit of a devil.

And clergymen, loving permissive society,
Sample its ties in alarming variety,
Stick out their necks, with a fervour hysterical,
Seeking a yoke that is wholly unclerical.

So people nostalgic, who love pious gloom,
And want a religion that reeks of the tomb,
Should only accept with a worthy esteem,
The parson engulfed in a jampot supreme.

Those keen ecumenicals, merging their borders,
Are wasting their time on the question of Orders;
For now we've discovered the source of validity,
Plainly defined with a perfect lucidity.

Now it is patently clear to the scholar,
That Clergyman-Power resides in the collar,
Which somehow imparts to the clerical station,
A characteristic transmogrification.

S. J. Forrest

"Mind you . . . *if* I could afford it, and *if* I could be sure it'd get through to the people who *really* need it . . ."

A sermon should be like a mini-skirt — short enough to be interesting, but long enough to cover the subject.

"I am indignant to find that some people still repeat a certain old slander on middle-aged clergy. This alleges that some of them evade work by only preparing one sermon on Sunday, and then make it sound like two different ones, by preaching it in the morning with their teeth in, and in the evening with their dentures removed."

(Letter to a newspaper)

Definition of the "Safe Period" — Vatican Roulette.

A vicar was a Doctor of Divinity, while his wife was a Doctor of Medicine. Someone called at the vicarage and asked to see the Doctor. The housekeeper asked: "Do you want the one who practises or the one who preaches?"

When Yuri Gagarin returned from the first ever manned flight into space he was greeted by Nikita Kruschev in person. After the customary bear-hug, Kruschev took the astronaut aside to his study and said: "Tell me Comrade Yuri, when you were up there in the vastness of space, did you by any chance sense the existence of that entity which the Capitalists call 'God'?"

Somewhat embarrassed, Gagarin replied: "Well, Comrade Kruschev, since you ask me, I have to admit that I did."

Kruschev looked concerned and then said: "Now listen Comrade; *you* know this and *I* know this, but for reasons of higher policy you must never breath a word of it to a living soul."

Shortly afterwards, Gagarin set off on a world tour.

In due course he arrived at the Vatican where the Pope took him aside for the most private of audiences.

"Tell me Captain Gagarin," he said, "when you were up there in the vastness of space, did you not sense the existence of that Entity which we call 'God'."

And Gagarin, remembering his promise to Kruschev, replied: "No, Your Holiness, I did not."

"Now listen Captain," said the Pope, "you know this and I know this, but for reasons of higher policy, you must never breath a word of it to a living soul."

A South London clergyman received a letter from a firm of furniture removers, who approached him on his appointment to a new living, stating: "In the last year we have removed forty South London clergymen to the entire satisfaction of all concerned."

The bride's dear old aunt sent a telegram to be read at the reception. It simply said: "1 John 4:18" (Perfect love casteth out fear).

But the Post Office transcribed it as John 4:18 so what was read out was: "Thou hast had five husbands, and he whom thou now hast is not thine husband."

A little girl had a cross-eyed teddy bear of which she was very fond. She proudly showed it to some visiting friends, and said its name was "Gladly".

"Why do you call it Gladly?" she was asked.

"Because we sing about it in church," she said.

The visitors were puzzled, and asked when that happened.

"Oh," said the little girl, "we often sing a hymn called 'Gladly my cross-eyed bear'."

Three sons went home on holiday; two were priests and one was a rip-roaring scoundrel. They all had dreams in the night. When they came down in the morning, Dad said: "What did you dream about?"

The first priest said: "Oh, Heaven. It was just like home here."

"Good boy," said Dad. "Come and stand on the hearth by me."

Exactly the same thing occurred with the second priest. Then down came the third son, bleary-eyed and yawning. "What did you dream about, son?"

"Oh, I dreamed about Hell."

"Hell?" said Dad.

"Yes," said the son. "It was just like home, nobody could get near the fire for priests."

Sunday school teacher: "What must you do before you obtain forgiveness of sin?"
   Child: "Sin."

An old vicar had passed his eightieth birthday and had been in his parish over thirty years. For years past he had been growing increasingly doddery and forgetful. The Rural Dean was in despair, the Archdeacon was in despair. At length the Bishop wrote him a tactful letter gently suggesting that it was time he took a well-earned rest.

Back came the indignant reply: "When your Lordship's last predecessor but three appointed me to this living, there was no mention of it being a temporary appointment."

A picture in a recent issue of the *Chicago Tribune* carried this caption: "Monsignors John L. May, William E. McManus and Thomas J. Grady pictured after their appointment as auxiliary bishops. Full story on Obituary page."

A schoolboy was asked to give an example of moral courage. He said: "If there were ten boys sleeping in a dormitory and one of them knelt down to say his prayers, while the others did not, that would be an example of moral courage. But if, on the other hand, ten bishops were sleeping in a dormitory and one of them did not kneel down to say his prayers, that would likewise be an example of moral courage."

One Sunday three Protestant ladies were obliged to take shelter in a village R.C. church in Eire. The priest, knowing them by sight, and wishing to show respect, whispered to his server: "Three chairs for the Protestant ladies."

The server jumped to his feet and shouted: "Three cheers for the Protestant ladies!"

The congregation rose, responded heartily, and the service proceeded.

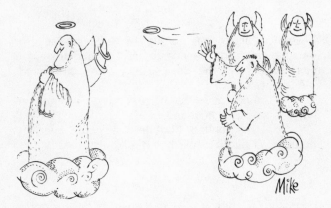

The late President Eisenhower's interpreter illustrated the perils of literal translation with a story about the interpreting machine that could handle 40,000 words in English and the equivalent in another language. The test sentence was: "The spirit is willing but the flesh is weak." This came out: "The liquor is still good but the meat has gone bad."

Brigitte Bardot arrived at the Pearly Gates and was greeted by a suprised Saint Peter. "Yours is a doubtful case," he said. "I shall have to take you into the Bureau for Doubtful Admissions." The Bureau was at the end of a long passage, and Saint Peter gave careful instructions. "Go carefully," he said, "for if you think a single naughty thought on the way, the floor will open, and you will fall straight down to the other place."

Miss Bardot set off down the passage, with Saint Peter following close behind. Suddenly the floor opened and Saint Peter fell straight through.

A young curate was taking his wife to task for breaking her promise not to buy a new dress. "It must have been the devil's fault," she murmured. "He tempted me."

"You could have said: 'Get thee behind me Satan'," said her husband.

"I did," she replied, "but he whispered over my shoulder: 'It fits you just beautifully at the back'."

In Ghana, in 1958, I was being driven round Accra in a taxi. The driver, a Northern Territory man, was pointing out the sights, including the many churches.

"Are you a Christian yourself?" I asked.

"No, no; myself I am a Presbyterian," he replied.

Parson's wife to husband, waking him at 1.30 a.m.: "I can't get to sleep tonight, read me one of your sermons dear."

An Irish Catholic priest was told that a man had arrived in the parish to work on a farm several miles away, and that he had fourteen children. Full of enthusiasm the priest dashed off on his bicycle to visit the man. "Well," he said, "it's a pleasure to welcome you, and to know that you have these fourteen lovely children, all to the Glory of God."

"But, Father," said the main, "I'm not a Catholic."

"Goodness," cried the priest. "To think I came all this way just for a sex-maniac."

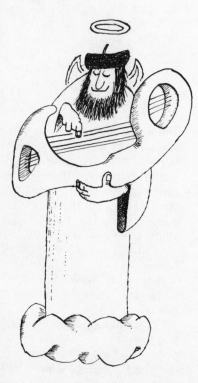

The priest teed off at the putting green, and scored a perfect hole-in-one. His opponent, Paddy, decided that he would not be beaten and took great care over his shot. With a near-perfect stroke he hit the ball which landed only a foot from the hole, rolled on and stopped only an inch away.

"Christ, I missed the * * * * ," yelled Paddy.

"My son," said the priest, "that is blasphemy. You should say: "Oh dear, I've missed it."

"I'll remember that, Father," replied Paddy.

For his next "tee-off" the priest executed another superb hole-in-one. Paddy, determined not to be beaten, made an excellent attempt, but his ball stopped only half an inch from the hole.

"Christ, I missed the * * * *," he yelled.

"My son," retorted the priest, "if you blaspheme again a flash of lightning will come from the sky and smite you dead."

"I'll remember that, Father," replied Paddy.

At the third hole the priest repeated his success with another hole-in-one.

Paddy teed off carefully, but the ball stopped a quarter of an inch from the hole.

"Christ, I've missed the * * * *," yelled Paddy.

Suddenly a flash of lightning came from the sky which struck the priest.

The Irishman looked on in horror while the priest fell to the ground, and a voice came from the sky: "Christ, I've missed the * * * *."

A certain vicar had a company of gipsies encamped in a field near his church. They left suddenly one night, leaving behind them a half-buried dead donkey. The vicar telephoned the local Borough Council about it. The official who answered, being something of a wag, replied that he always understood that it was the duty of a vicar to bury the dead. The vicar retorted at once: "That may be so, but I thought it was at least my duty to inform the relatives of the deceased!"

Benevolent old lady: "Have you any religious convictions?"

Tramp: "Not worth mentioning, lady, but I got a month once for stealing an almsbox."

The motorist stopped his car and asked the clergyman who was walking along the country lane whether he could offer him a lift. Very pre-occupied, the clergyman replied: "That's very kind of you, but I'm afraid I should have no use for such a gift. You see I live in a bungalow."

A clergyman was prejudiced against the use of Latin, and would never use the phrase *Deo Volente* — usually abbreviated to "D.V.", but always said "God willing" or "G.W." He wrote a card to a friend, at whose church he was going to preach, saying: "I hope to arrive at Barnstable, G.W., at noon next Saturday." The reply was a telegram: "Don't come by G.W., the Southern Railway station is nearer."

George, age six, was a farmer's son, and one Sunday, his parents entertained the local preacher. When a visitor called at the farm the next day, George was full of the news. "We had a locust preacher to tea yesterday."

"I think you mean the *local* preacher, George. A locust is a thing that eats everything that's put before it."

"Yes," said George, "this one did."

Three Scotsmen went to Mass one Sunday morning. When the plate came round for the offering, one Scotsman fainted, and the other two carried him out.

Two old maids were making their plans for Christmas. "Mary," asked the younger, "do you think one long wide stocking would hold all you want for Christmas?"

"No, May," replied the other with a sigh, "but a pair of socks would."

Vicar, to his friend, a factory manager: "Your factory hooter keeps good time. Do you set it by Big Ben?"

"No," was the reply, "we set it by your church clock. Do you set your church clock by Big Ben?"

"No," answered the Vicar, "we set it by your hooter."

A bishop presented the prizes at a well known public school. Afterwards the Headmaster said: "I hope you will stay for the evening; the boys are giving 'Much ado about Nothing'."

"Thank you very much," replied the bishop, "but I've just had three days at the Church Assembly."

A Scotsman was met by Peter at the Gates of Heaven.

"Tell me, son, what have you done to deserve entry into Heaven?"

"Well, I'm a Roman Catholic."

"That's a help of course, but not enough. What good deeds have you performed?"

The Scotsman scratched his head. Then: "I rescued a drowning child from the frozen Clyde."

"That's quite commendable, but not enough."

"I am a Celtic supporter, and I stood at the Rangers' end on Cup Final day, wearing my Celtic scarf, right in the middle of all the heathens."

"That's very brave," said Saint Peter, obviously moved. "When was that?"

"I'm not quite sure, but I would say less than half-an-hour ago."

A teacher had been telling her class the story of Noah and the Ark. She asked them if they could suggest how Noah spent his time during the flood. There being no reply, she said: "Don't you think he did a lot of fishing?"

"No, miss," replied one of the bright ones, "I don't think he did."

"Why don't you think he did a lot of fishing then?" smiled the teacher.

"Because," replied the boy, "he had only two worms."

Dictum of Saint Theresa: "Lord, if you treat your friends like this, no wonder you have so few!"

A certain clergyman is said to have written to his bishop to ask if he could marry himself, as he wished the wedding to be very quiet, and did not want to trouble any other clergyman. The bishop is said to have replied that he could not give him permission to marry himself, but he thought he might allow him to bury himself if he wished and felt able.

A young clergyman had preached what he thought was an outstanding sermon. He asked one of the older members of the congregation whether he had enjoyed it. "No, I did not," replied the old man in a very firm tone.

"What was wrong with it?" asked the clergyman, rather taken aback.

"Weel, in the first place it was read, in the second place it wasna weel read, and in the third place it wasna worth reading."

"But Lent is a period of *giving* also — and not only to the Chancellor of the Exchequer . . ."

After a tiring day the Bishop decided to go for a walk in the forest. There he met a tiger. Straight away he knelt down to pray, and peeped through his fingers only to see that the tiger was also kneeling, with paws over his eyes.

"What are you doing?" asked the Bishop.

"Saying my Grace," said the tiger.

"How utterly pointless," said the Gothic arch on first seeing a Norman one.

Two churches were opposite each other. Outside one church was a notice saying: "Drink is man's worst enemy."

Outside the other was a notice saying: "Make your worst enemy your best friend."

Mrs D. M. Castell writes: "Some time ago I was trying to phone our Bishop to thank him for an invitation to tea. After several fruitless attempts I finally dialled Directory Enquiries and said I was trying to get the Bishop of Leeds. 'Hang on a mo,' said the girl, 'I'll try and find out.' I waited a minute or so, and read your letter in the *Catholic Herald* about your forthcoming book of ecclesiastical fun. Imagine my delight when the operator returned and said: 'I'm sorry love, but I've looked up every Public House in the town, and I can't find the Bishop of Leeds'."

One of the most complete sets of records of marine disasters is kept in the library of a certain American Insurance Company. Its completeness is so legendary that it is said that someone wrote to ask for information about Noah's Ark. In due course this reply was received: "Built in 2448 B.C. Gopher wood coated with pitch within and without. Length 300 cubits; width 50 cubits; height 30 cubits. Three decks. Cattle carrier. Owner: Noah and Sons. Last reported stranded Mount Ararat."

A business tycoon in conversation with the late Dr Parker, said: "I am a self-made man."

"I am glad to hear it, sir." retorted Parker, "You have lifted a great responsibility from the shoulders of the Almighty."

There used to be a church in Maiden Lane in which there was a passage running from the organ loft to the bar of the pub next door. At the midday service the organist normally spent the period of the sermon having a drink or two. On one occasion he over-

stayed his drinking time, and returned to hear the congregation singing the hymn after the sermon unaccompanied. Thinking quickly the organist took his coat off, smeared his hands with grease, and in a dishevelled condition, reported to the vicar after the service. "It won't happen again," he said. "It took some time, but I found the faulty pipe."

A church minister received, among other Christmas presents, a bottle of cherry brandy from one of his parishioners. Wishing to thank the parishioner without drawing attention to the exact nature of the present, the minister gave out the following notice from the pulpit.

"I have been so very pleased with all your Christmas wishes, with so many cards and so many presents. Especially do I wish to thank one friend for his gift of fruit, and the spirit in which it was given."

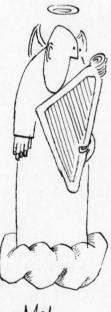

Mike

An official of the Vatican Secretariat for Christian Unity was at Lambeth Palace making arrangements for the visit of the Archbishop of Canterbury to the Pope. When the discussion turned to travel the visitor promised that prayers for the Archbishop's safe arrival would be offered by the Secretariat's President, Cardinal Bea.

"Pray, assure his Eminence," replied Dr Ramsey, "that I have every confidence in B.E.A."

An R.A.F. sergeant who had been shot down over France, landed safely by parachute near a convent, and was given asylum by the nuns. Walking in the convent garden by the side of a nun who appeared particularly attractive, he made coy advances; these were responded to in a deep gruff voice which said: "Don't be a bloody fool, I've been here since Dunkirk."

A young and newly appointed bishop arrived at the Cathedral door for his induction ceremony. When he knocked on the door it was opened by a number of aged and very decrepit canons. Turning to his chaplain, the bishop murmured: "The see throws up its dead!"

The members of a chapel met to discuss the question of repairs to the ceiling. A wealthy member stood up and said he would give £5. As he sat down a piece of ceiling fell on his head. He rose again and said he would make it £50. Thereupon a good brother shouted; "Hit him again, Lord."

"It would make a marvellous bowling alley."

A small girl was taken to her first wedding ceremony. Afterwards, she said to her mother: "I think that lady changed her mind, because she went up the aisle with one man, and came down with another."

An I.R.A. man arrived at the Gates of Heaven with a large pack of gelignite. "Away with you," said Saint Peter. "You can't come in here!"

"I don't want to come in," said the I.R.A. man. "I'm giving you four minutes to get out."

A church in Mayfair has a notice board outside it. On the board is written: "If you are tired of sin, come inside." Underneath this is scrawled: "And if you're not ring 727 8106."

A country rector, who had just announced his impending retirement, was visiting an elderly parishioner. As he thought of his happy years in the parish, he remarked: "Yes God has been very good to me."

"But don't forget," replied the lady, "you have been very good to God."

Pat and his old pal were walking home after Mass. The Gospel they had heard was about the Pharisees and the Publican. "Well, John," said Pat, "thank God we're not like them Pharisees."

Pope John XXIII once visited the Holy Ghost Hospital in Rome. The Mother Superior, beaming with joy, introduced herself: "Holy Father, I am the Superior of the Holy Ghost."

Pope John replied with a smile: "I am only the representative of Christ."

Two nuns were travelling up to London one day in a red mini. On arrival, one nun went off to do some shopping. When she returned, both the car and the other nun were missing. "Excuse me," she said to a policeman, "have you seen a nun in a red mini?"

"No," said the policeman, "but I wouldn't be surprised at anything nowadays."

In a Trappist monastery it was permitted that every member of the community could speak on Easter Sunday once every seven years. When it came to Brother Alberic's turn he complained that his bed was excessively uncomfortable. The Abbot promised to look into the matter. Seven years later it was Alberic's turn to utter again and once again he complained about the bed. "If you've only complained about it twice in fourteen years," remarked the Abbot, "it can't be as bad as all that!"

Typical of the less ecumenical days of my youth was the old chestnut about the Reverend Mother who asked several of the girls in her school what they proposed to do with their lives. The first said she would be a nurse, the second a mother with several children, the third a school teacher and so on.

All were commended for the wisdom of their choice until it came to the last girl who said she would like to be a prostitute. Greatly shocked, the nun asked her to repeat what she had said.

"I want to be a prostitute," said the girl.

"A WHAT?" said the nun.

"I said a PROSTITUTE."

"Heaven be praised," cried the nun. "For one awful moment I thought you said 'Protestant'!"

Mary, aged about seven, was attending a church service with her mother, when she complained that she felt unwell. Her mother, told her to go outside, and to be sure to go right round the back of the church garden. Afterwards her mother asked what had happened because Mary was no sooner gone than she was back again.

"Oh it was all right, Mummy," she said, "I didn't have to go outside. When I got to the porch, I saw a box marked 'for the sick'."

A boy in Sunday School was asked who was the first man. He promptly replied: "Adam." On being asked who was the first woman, he hesitatingly replied: "Madam."

"Official Programme — going cheap . . ."

Two men were praying ardently in church. One was obviously well-to-do praying for the success of his investments. The other was poor and was praying for a windfall of £20 to pay his back rent.

Said number one: "What's the trouble, my friend?"

Number two told him, whereupon the well-to-do man replied: "Here, take this £20, pay your rent, and have an easy mind."

With many thanks the other left the church.

Our benefactor returned to his prayers. "And now, Lord," he said, "may I have your undivided attention?"

Oh Vicar, I cannot go reading tonight,
I haven't a thing I can wear!
My surplice no longer is whiter than white,
And I need a blue rinse in my hair;
My lay-reader's scarf is of last year's hue,
My cassock, a positive rogue!
I cannot perform till I've studied the norm,
In the "Readers Edition" of Vogue.

The unisex garment, supplied by the Church,
All discrimination deters,
Unless it's embroidered in legible script,
Emblazoned with HIS or with HERS;
The staircarpet scarf that we wear round the neck,
Is hardly an object of joy;
But surely it ought to be pink for a girl,
And blue in the case of a boy?

The Young Readers' Conference harps on the theme,
Of the varying hem of the cassock;
The mini, or midi, which float in the air,
Or the maxi which trails on the hassock.
Our mighty cathedral, with elegant choir,
Is entranced by the gayest of sights;
The Lord Bishop's wife in her miniest robes,
And her sky-blue diocesan tights.

Though some like to dress in the guise of a man,
In places where Anglicans pray
Still more would uphold the feminine right
To remain ornamental and gay;
So the practice of modelling readers' robes,
Could become quite a novel vocation,
As the corsetry firms find a part they can play
In the Church's newest foundation.

S. J. Forrest

The Collection

"The parson looks it o'er and frets;
It puts him out of sorts,
To see how many times he gets,
A penny for this thoughts."

Two chaps met after many years, having been at Ecclesiastical College together. One had become a bishop, the other was a parish priest. They were discussing their differing ways of life and the parish priest said to the bishop: "It's all right for you, you only have to have one really good sermon and you can go round the country preaching it again and again, whereas I have to preach a different sermon every week."

To this the bishop replied that of course he did not agree and that he was quite capable of preaching on any subject, and if his old friend would like to write some words and put them on the pulpit he would preach them that evening.

It came to the time for the sermon at Evensong, the bishop went into the pulpit and looked down at the slip of paper. It carried one word: "Constipation".

The bishop looked round the congregation and said: "My text tonight is 'Moses took the tablets and went into the wilderness'."

(Derek Nimmo)

"I know, son — they *were* only two by two when they came aboard!"

An Irish lorry-driver asked advice about an interview for a new job in the North East. He was told that everything depended on his knowing that part of the country. The prospective employer asked if he knew Stockton-on-Tees. Yes indeed. Darlington? Like the back of his hand. Northallerton? His grandmother lived there.

"And what about York?"

"Sir, that was where I was married."

"Bishop Auckland?"

"Him? Why, he married us!"

A Scotsman was visiting Lake Galilee, and asked how much a boat-trip cost. When he was told £100, he said he was not surprised that Jesus walked.

"We have a mad priest in the Psychiatric Ward," said the Reverend Mother to the Abbot. "He has been telling his congregations the most terrible things and it has become an embarrassment to the Cardinal. He has been preaching on subjects like sin. Well, we all know there's no such thing as sin. Syndromes yes, but sin . . . No!"

"Daddio"

Pushed through the front door was a duplicated notice about the Scouts' jumble sale. The first two sentences read as follows:

A chance to get rid of anything not quite worth keeping but too good to throw away. Don't forget to bring your husbands.

"Here's a couple of quid . . . try next door . . ."

"Do you say your prayers before you eat?" the priest asked the little boy.

"I don't need to, Father," replied the child, "my mother is a good cook."

A man went to Brompton Oratory to go to Confession. He knelt down beside the Confessional and, hearing a slight rustle from behind the grating, began his confession. "Bless me Father for I have sinned", and so on.

His confession lasted quite a while and then there was a lengthy silence. He began to feel uncomfortable. Was the priest, perhaps, so horrified at the recital that he couldn't speak?

The penitent coughed nervously and then pressed his face close to the grille to peer through. Dismayed he saw that the slight noise heard previously had come, not from the priest's compartment, but from a waiting penitent who was kneeling, fidgeting on the far side of the box.

"I say," he called through the grating in a loud whisper, "excuse me, but could you tell me where the priest is?"

"I don't know," came the reply, "but, from what I've just heard, I should think he's gone to fetch the police!"

Pope John, on being asked how many people worked in the Vatican, is said to have answered: "I would think about half."

The nuns badly needed £100. The novices prayed hard to Saint Joseph. They left a petition at the foot of his statue — but with no result.

They put the petition in Saint Joseph's hands; still no result.

They were given permission to add spectacles to Saint Joseph. Then came the Bishop's visitation and the Novice sisters thought the spectacles had better be removed. But Reverend Mother said: "No, leave them. Should his Lordship notice, I'll explain."

The Bishop did notice. "What's this, what's this?" Reverend Mother explained. "What," said the Bishop. "Take away those spectacles — what superstition! I'll give you the £100."

An eighteenth-century bishop had a country house which he never visited. A friend asked if he might be allowed to take it on lease. "My dear friend," replied the bishop, "I fear you do not understand. One must always have a place to which one does not in fact go, but where one believes one would be happy if one did."

"Quite so," said the friend, "that is what has made the reputation of Heaven."

A Bible class leader was asked how far it actually was from Dan to Bathsheba, as quoted in the Old Testament. "I never realised those were actual place-names," said another member. "I thought they were husband and wife, like Sodom and Gomorrah."

A Biblical epic film had a break in the middle. During this, ladies came round with trays of Bibles. They were intermissionaries.

Sister had been explaining the meaning of prefixes to a class of young children.
" 'Trans' means 'across'. Now what does 'transistor' mean?"
    Bright boy: "I know: 'a cross nun'."

A curate who had not long been ordained had to carry out his first cremation ceremony and was told that the Vicar could not accompany him to show him what to do. The crematorium was rather old-fashioned: when the button was pressed for the committal, the floor opened and the coffin descended. The curate was nervous, and had to press a number of buttons before arriving at the one for the committal.
    Somewhat relieved that he had reached this stage of the service without any mistakes, he pressed the committal button with some force, and caused a short in the electricity. From where the congregation was standing there was a big blue flash, a puff of smoke, and the coffin had gone.
    One mourner was seen to turn to the next one and say: "Well, we know where he's gone, don't we."

Reading aloud during a scripture lesson Roger came to the passage: "Therefore with Angels and Archangels." He pronounced it "Angels and Dark Angels" and the class roared with laughter.

"Why all the fuss?" said Roger. "There is no colour bar in Heaven."

Two small sons of an Irish farmer were paying their first visit to London. They were fascinated by the traffic lights which they had never seen before, particularly by the brief period of the amber light as the signals changed.

"Glory be," exclaimed one, "they don't give the Protestants much time to cross."

Cardinal Godfrey, late Archbishop of Westminster, once told of his conversation with a lady who kept a repository. He asked how the medals were selling. She replied that holy medals always went well since many people bought them as charms. One purchaser once actually asked her directly: "Have you got any charms?" To which she answered: "No, not at my time of life."

A farmer invited the visiting preacher to a meal after the morning service. During the week he had killed two cockerels, one for this meal and the other for his own family's supper. However, the preacher brought a clerical friend with him, and, owing to their large appetites, both fowls were eaten. Afterwards the farmer showed his visitors round the farmyard. One of them was struck by the sight of a cock crowing lustily. "That's a fine bird you have," he said, "he seems mighty proud of himself."

Said the farmer, "And well he might be; he's just had two sons entered the Ministry!"

Father Faber, the Victorian composer
of many pious Catholic hymns, wrote
the following last two lines on the
occasion of an important feast-day in
Rome:—

    "The Holy Father's eyes were dim,
    The Feast had been too much for
                            him."

A small Protestant girl, Joan, and her Catholic friend James, both aged four, were swimming in a pond with nothing on. James looked at Joan, and shouted in surprise. "So that's the difference between Protestants and Catholics."

During the processional hymn, the heel of a girl chorister caught in a grating. Not wishing to hold up the ceremony, she marched on, minus shoe. Moved by chivalry, a male chorister, following, tried to pick up the shoe. Unfortunately the heel was stuck firmly in the grating, so, again not wanting to hold up the procession, the chorister picked up the whole lot, and continued up the nave. The officiating clergyman behind promptly fell into the hole.

A Baptist Minister preaching by invitation in a Jewish synagogue, was alarmed to see strange looks of anguish on the faces of the congregation when he mentioned Moses.

After the service, he asked the Rabbi for an explanation. "Ah," said the Rabbi, "Moses is in disfavour with us at the moment; has been for some time. You see, if only Moses had turned right instead of left when he came out of the Red Sea, we would now be selling oil, instead of grapefruit and oranges."

Incidentally, Mrs Meir made the same comment, in slightly different terms, to M. Pompidou on a recent visit.

Although I'm Church of England,
I haven't been of late,
Since organized religion
Is somewhat out of date;
With desiccated clergy,
And fossil-forms of prayer,
Which fail to bring conviction,
Or lead us anywhere.
I never went to worship,
Since everybody said
The Church was quite outdated,
And almost wholly dead.
'Twas plain its aged structure
Was riddled with decay,
And in an early future
Would surely pass away.

I went to Church at Christmas
In sentimental mood,
To rouse nostalgic echoes
On bygone days to brood;
But horror rose on horror,
And left my mind deranged,
For services had altered,
And everything was changed!
The noble rites of Cranmer,
The fine old B.C.P.
Had now been superseded,
As far as I could see;
A crowded congregation,
Equipped with books of blue,
Were ploughing through a service,
Described as "Series Two".

The rights of every voter
To find his Church the same,
Are cynically flouted
By such a Christmas game;
These words, so unfamiliar,
The language, stark and bare,
All blatantly unsuited
For Anglicans at prayer.
If changes thus continue,
We confidently state,
The Church of England structure
Will soon disintegrate,
As clergymen, and vandals,
Injure her soul unique,
And thus destroy for ever
A valuable antique.

S. J. Forrest

A soldier went to a priest and said: "Father, I need your help. I've got two girls at home, Maria and Susan, and I can't decide which one to marry. What can I do?"

The priest replied: "Well, there's nothing that I can say except advise you to go and pray."

So the soldier went off, only to return to the priest half an hour later, jubilant. "Father, it worked. I went into the church and knelt down and prayed, and when I looked up, right in front of my eyes were the words 'ave Maria', so I've written to Maria and told 'er I'll marry 'er on my next leave, and I've given Susan the brush-off."

"Isn't it shocking, My Lord," said the over-serious curate to the visiting bishop, "how the young people today think nothing of pre-marital intercourse. I didn't sleep with my wife before we were married, did you My Lord?"

"I don't know," said the Bishop, giving him a distant look. "What was her maiden name?"

Pat on his way home, drunk as usual, met the parish priest.

Priest: "Drunk again Pat?"

Pat: "So am I, Father."

Notice given out one Sunday: "A lady's wristwatch has been found in the church. Please will the owner come to the Vicarage after the service. We will now sing Hymn No 362: "Lord, her watch thy church is keeping."

A teacher died, and went to Heaven. He arrived at the "pearly gates," knocked, and waited to be admitted. When the gates opened, to his horror he was confronted, not by Saint Peter, but by the Devil.

"Good Lord!" he said. "Have I come to the wrong place?"

"No," replied the Devil. "Don't worry; we've just gone comprehensive."

Three nuns out walking together were discussing what each would do if she found a £5 note in the road.

One said she would give it to the convent. Another promised it to the foreign missions. The third, a young sister, said she would give it to the first poor person that she saw.

Before they had gone very far, this last nun did in fact find such a note, and seeing a tramp-like figure loitering on the pavement, she thrust the note into his hand, bidding him "God speed".

The next day, the portress at the convent was surprised to find this same character at the door asking for the young nun. His description was too vague and the portress was hesitant.

"It's most important that you find her," said the man. "Yesterday she gave me £5 to put on 'God Speed', and it romped home at fifty to one."

"But officer . . . how was I to know that someone was going to mix Cannabis Resin in the Incense?"

A Presbyterian Minister was called on at short notice to officiate at the parish church of Craithrie at a service attended by Queen Victoria. He was so overcome with the importance of the occasion that he came out with this prayer:

"Grant that as she grows to be an old woman, she be made a new man, and stand before thee as a pure virgin, bringing forth sons and daughters to thy glory; and that in all peaceful causes she may go before her people like a he-goat on the mountain."

He was never asked to officiate again.

The Cardinal looked in the looking glass. Yes, he thought, that would do. He was wearing a nice new Cardinal Red trouser suit and a white tie as it was pascal time. He was going to a rehearsal of his television show; this would show the country that the Church was up to date. He gave himself a squish of the new toilet water for men, a preparation made to his order and aimed especially at the clerical market. It was called "Eau de Sanctite". He had already applied the other preparation which he plugged on his show, "Deodorant de Sanctite". Rather nice, he thought, sniffing. It had a faint whiff of incense.

"Daddio"

Tommy and his mother arrived a little late, and the minister was already in the pulpit — one of those with a door leading into the main body of the church. All went well till the sermon, when the minister became — at least to Tommy — more agitated. He thumped the lectern, waved his arms and shouted at the congregation. Tommy was very worried, and catching his mother's arm, asked anxiously: "What do we do if he gets out?"

"Make room, Luv!"

The lady, standing rather nervously on the platform of the country railway station, was waiting to meet a visiting local preacher, who was entirely unknown to her. At last the train arrived and approaching one of the few passengers to leave it, she enquired rather hesitantly: "Excuse me, but are you the local Methodist preacher?"

"No lady, I'm not. It's me rheumatism that makes me look as I do."

"At the Lincoln county picnic in Vineland, Ontario, the rolling-pin contest was won by Mrs W. H. Upsall, the vicar's wife, who threw it 67 feet. Mr Upsall won the hundred yards dash for married men."

(from a newspaper report)

During the Second Vatican Council a young man approached a bishop outside Saint Peter's, claiming he was a theologian, and asked the bishop if he would take him into the Council as his theological expert. The bishop readily agreed and together they entered.

At the end of the session the young man bade the bishop farewell and said: "It is only fair to tell you, my Lord, that I'm not really a theologian, but a journalist."

"That's perfectly all right," said the bishop. "In fact, I'm a journalist myself; robes can be hired quite cheaply from a place near the Piazza Colonna."

Child: "I'm drawing a picture of God."
 Mother: "But nobody knows what God looks like, dear."
 Child: "They will when I've finished."

The little son of the house had always taken the collection very seriously, and in no circumstances would have thought of going to church without his penny. There came a Sunday, however, when he noticed that a guest in the family had come unprovided. Sliding along the seat towards her, he whispered: "Where's your penny?"

"I didn't bring one," came the reply.

"Here," said the gallant little man, "take mine. I'll get under the seat."

Sixty years ago in Brazil, in places where there was no church, the Anglican Bishop often had to give services in the house of a British resident. On one such occasion he was to hold a Communion Service, and the Japanese butler of the house was instructed to prepare some wine and some sliced bread cut into squares.

The butler, accustomed to cocktail parties, said he understood what was wanted, and a decanter of wine and a covered dish were set on the table. The small congregation assembled, and at the appropriate stage of the service, the Bishop lifted the cover from the dish. The squares of bread were there according to instructions and on each one was a small piece of anchovy.

The following news item appeared recently in the Northampton *Mercury and Herald:* "The Rev W. T. Hunter is vacating the pulpit of Rothwell Congregational Church, which he has occupied for ten years."

"Will ladies responsible for making tea kindly empty tea-pots and kettles, then stand upside down in the sink."

(Notice in Nottinghamshire Church Hall)

An exasperated salesman abandoned his car in a non-parking zone and left a note saying: "I've circled this block twenty times. I have an appointment to keep and must get to it. Forgive us our trespasses."

He returned to find a parking ticket under his wiper-blade and another note attached: "I've circled this block for twenty years. If I don't book you I'll lose my job. Lead us not into temptation."

An altar-boy was reproved by the priest for being late at the church. "Please Father," said the lad, "the traffic was terrible and my Dad says it's better to be late than dead on time . . ."

A mother had been having trouble getting her young son to attend Sunday School. So, she tried psychology. She read her young man the story of the Pilgrim Fathers when they landed in America, telling him how the Pilgrims attended church under

the most difficult conditions. "The Pilgrims never missed church on Sunday," his mother pointed out.

"I'd go to Sunday School every Sunday too," the youngster snapped, "if you would let me carry a gun and shoot Indians on the way."

"No, Eminence, not a flying saucer, merely the natural exuberance of some of the young new Cardinals."

A Bishop was spending a holiday in the country and was persuaded to speak at a church meeting. The Churchwarden, in proposing a vote of thanks, said how honoured they all were by the presence of such a distinguished visitor. "In fact a poorer speaker would have been quite good enough for us, but we couldn't find one."

A small boy was exasperating his mother. She said to him: "You are a naughty boy. How do you expect to get into Heaven if you behave like this?"

He replied: "I shall go up to the pearly gates and rush in and out, and in and out, and I shall bang them and won't wipe my feet and Saint Peter will come out of his little lodge, and will say to me: 'For goodness sake, boy, either come in or go out', and I shall go in."

A demure young lady was asked by a modern young man whether she believed every word of the Bible.

"Yes," she replied, "I do."

"Surely," exclaimed the young man, "you don't believe that Jonah was swallowed by a whale, and that Elijah was fed by ravens?"

"I do," she answered, "and when I get to Heaven I'll ask them about it."

"But suppose they are not in Heaven?" enquired the young man with a sneer.

"Then you'll be able to ask them," was the young lady's reply.

Further . . .   proof . . .

of the efficacy . . .   of prayer.

A company director went to Hell and was greeted by the Devil. "Come with me," he said. "I've reserved as good a place as I could for you."

On the way they passed a group sitting in apparently perfect comfort in a club-room. "They look very comfortable," said the newcomer. "Could I join them?"

"Good Heavens, no," said the Devil, "those are your shareholders; they're all too green to burn."

Acquaintance Preserved

"And so, my dear old Service friend, goodbye, and may God pickle you." — End of letter, written with the aid of a dictionary, from a Belgian to a Londoner he got to know during the war.

"How is your wife's cold?" asked Father Finnegan when he met Cassidy on the street.

"She hasn't got a cold," said Cassidy.

"But she was coughing very badly in church on Sunday. Everybody was looking round at the poor woman."

"That was no cold," said Cassidy. "She just wanted them to see the new hat she's bought."

An Irish priest was giving instructions to a class of small girls at Sunday school.

"You shouldn't be watching T.V. and listening to pop records all the time. What do you think Our Lady was doing—was she wasting her time? No, she was on her knees, saying the Rosary."

A Bishop who had a premonition that he would be smitten with a stroke, used to pinch his leg to know if it had come. At a luncheon party once, he tried pinching, and, not feeling it, cried out: "It's come, it's come."

The lady sitting beside him remarked: "Excuse me, Sir, but you are pinching my leg."

"This'll fox 'em . . . *looks* like a Dove . . . flies like a Dove . . . and packs three times the bomb load of a B.29!"

Moses spoke to his P.R. saying that he wanted good publicity when crossing the Red Sea.

Moses: "What will you give me if I build a bridge?"

P.R.: "No sorry, can't do anything for that."

Moses: "I could make a raft."

P.R.: "Maybe a column on the back page."

Moses: "Open the waters?"

P.R.: "Better—yes, I could get you a page in the Bible for that."

Christ Church, West Bromwich, has a wide expanse of church yard fronting the local High Street, and in bad winter weather, the task of clearing snow is a formidable one.

Many years ago, after a particularly heavy fall of snow, the Verger and general handyman was disinclined to wield a spade, and the snow remained on the ground. A policeman duly arrived on the scene and requested that the snow be cleared forthwith.

The Verger refused and said: "Who's supposed to clear the snow from the premises—the occupiers, aren't they?" The policeman agreed, and the Verger went on: "And who's the occupiers here? Them that are in the graves: let them clear it."

The fine was paid from Church funds.

Monastic Christmas

Mike

The Sunday School teacher was telling the story of the prodigal son. "But in the midst of all this joy and excitement," she said, "there was one to whom the prodigal's return brought no happiness; one who hated the thought of attending the feast. Who was that?"

A small voice said: "The fatted calf."

An Irish priest offered sixpence to the boy who could tell him who was the greatest man in history. "Saint Patrick," shouted a bright little Jewish boy.

"The sixpence is yours," said the priest, "but how is it that you, a Jewish boy, have such a grand opinion of Saint Patrick?"

"Right down in my heart I knew it was Moses," answered the boy, "but business is business."

A clergyman called on an elderly lady who was deaf. When she expressed regret that she could not hear his sermons, he modestly and sympathetically said, "Oh, you don't miss much."

"So they tell me," she replied with a smile.

A bishop was consecrating a new church in Africa. The church was not fully furnished, so a soap-box was provided for the bishop to sit on. At one point in the service, the box collapsed, and the bishop fell to the floor. No one laughed, or took any notice. Afterwards, in the vestry, the bishop said: "What wonderful control your people showed!"

The local priest answered: "My lord, they thought it was part of the service."

An inspector examining a class in religious knowledge asked a little girl the following question, intending it to be a catch.

"What was the difference between Noah's Ark and Joan of Arc?"

He was a little surprised by the answer: "Noah's Ark was made of wood and Joan of Arc was maid of orleans."

A certain minister who was very fond of horseradish—the real thing, not the adulterated stuff that is half horseradish and half turnip—carried a bottle of it with him when he went on his holiday. While he was eating dinner in a hotel restaurant, another diner at the same table said he was from a far away country and was curious about the bottle in front of the minister's plate.

"Try some," said the minister.

The stranger needed no second invitation. He  placed some of the horseradish on his plate and then put a heaped spoonful in his mouth. His face immediately turned red, his eyes bulged, tears ran down his face. He swallowed convulsively two or three times, grabbed a glass of water, and then looking reproachfully at the minister, said: "I have known many men of God who preached hellfire and damnation, but you are the first I ever saw who carried a sample of it right along with him."

"Mind you — there's a lot to be said for being kicked *right* upstairs in this job . . ."

Tertullian, who is said to have promised the Christians the luxury of seeing their enemies roasting in the fires of Hell, has his followers. For instance, there was the old Methodist who walked out of a discussion on "Is there a Hell?" muttering "I *will* have my eternal punishment."

More recently, an Anglican brother said: "I won't give up my Hell. There are too many people I want to put into it."

Two merchant bankers appeared at the Pearly Gates. "This is a new one to me," said Saint Peter. "I must go and get instructions." When he came back the merchant bankers had gone — and so had the Pearly Gates.

A learned judge of my acquaintance told me that when he had been a young up-and-coming barrister he had sent his daughter to a certain well known convent school whose headmistress was a formidable nun with many aristocratic and cosmopolitan connections.

When his daughter had been at the school for a term or so, the headmistress asked him to call upon her. The barrister went in fear and trembling expecting to be asked to witness the public expulsion of his child.

Not so. On arrival he was taken into an innermost parlour where the headmistress requested his advice on a proposed financial transaction involving pounds and pesetas which "had I advised her to proceed," said my friend, "would certainly have landed her inside prison bars for a great many years to come!"

Two skeletons met in a churchyard. Said skeleton one: "How long have you been dead?"

Skeleton number two replied: "A hundred years. And how long have you been dead?"

To which number one answered: "I'm not dead. I'm the Curate."

A clergyman waiting for a train at Fleet, Hampshire, remarked to a junior porter on the number of people travelling by the train. "Yes," said the porter, "they work at the aircraft factory".

"Vickers?" asked the clergyman.

"No," was the reply, "ordinary blokes."

Question: "Who is the first man mentioned in the Bible?"

Answer: Please sir, Chap.I."

A bishop was preaching before the Mayor and Corporation of a certain town. During the sermon the Mayor took out a very large watch from his waistcoat and made no secret of consulting it. The bishop also rummaged beneath his robes and produced another large watch. "I make it ten past twelve," said the bishop, looking down from the pulpit. "What time do you make it?"

"Keep it up Brother Sigebert. . . . Keep it up!"

The young man at the doorstep asked the elderly occupant whether she was converted.

"I've been to more Church Services than you've had hot dinners," she snapped.

"Actually I'm from the Gas Board," he explained.

Q. Who made you?
A. God made me; why did he make *you*?

(Bishop Butler)

A Jew, Moslem and Christian were gambling clandestinely in a city where such activities were forbidden by law, when they were surprised by the police. They managed to hide all traces of evidence, but the police officer did not give up easily. He said: "I will let you off if each one of you will swear on oath that he was not playing cards."

"By . . . " swore the Moslem.

"By . . . " swore the Christian.

"Have you ever seen anyone playing cards alone?" said the Jew.

"So, of course, the moment I read the report, My Lord . . ."

The last trump.

Thanks are due to ...

Acknowledgements and thanks must be legion. Firstly to everybody of all ages and denominations who took the trouble to send in their suggestions even though I may not have been able to use them. To the newspapers who were kind enough to print my original letter and to the *Catholic Herald* and other publications and individuals who have allowed me to reprint my own and other drawings. To the BBC "Sunday" programme who broadcast an interview with me about the project and subsequently sent me the stories which their listeners had sent to them. To my daughter Marianne who applied her younger fresher wits to the problem of selection and prevented my, I hope, from being too old-fashioned. To Mayhew-McCrimmon who suggested and undertook the publication of the book.

Generally speaking I have included only items which made me laugh or smile or feel that there was a nice point somewhere. I am a Roman Catholic, but with a mother in the Church of Scotland and a wife in the Church of England, I hope I have managed to maintain an ecumenical balance. As it happens the most consistently funny stories seem to have come from the Baptists. But no joke can ever carry a guarantee of effectiveness.   I am particularly grateful to the Rev Michael Henesy who has allowed me to use many of his cartoons from *Novena* magazine. I had hoped to include a section  of favourite stories of distinguished people, but most of them, led by the Archbishop of Canterbury and the Editor of the *Times* have not surprisingly been unable for one reason or another to help. To those who wished me well I'm very grateful.

I must also thank Angela Cookson and Teresa Couldery for allowing me to include a number of extracts from "Daddio", an unpublished novel which satirises in ecclesiastical "Brave New World" style some of the more way-out activities of progressives within the Catholic Church. The printed episodes are incomplete in themselves but their witty descriptiveness will I hope add a touch of spice to what may otherwise be a somewhat mild concoction.

Very particular thanks are due to the Rev Conrad Ough who has been printing amusing anecdotes in his church magazine for many years and very kindly placed his unique scrapbook at my disposal. Mr Ough seems to have cornered most of the religious humour circulating in England over the last fifty years or so and I have borrowed a liberal selection from him. When I wrote asking him how he pronounced his name he replied: "There are nine different ways of pronouncing the letters OUGH in English. Ours is a Cornish family and we pronounce it 'Oh'. When I was appointed Curate at Tonbridge in 1932 there was a welcoming party so that parishioners could meet the new Curate. I was introduced by the Vicar who finished his remark by saying: 'And now you young ladies at the back, you can say what you like in his presence, but you mustn't say 'Oh dear'."

The author and publisher are grateful to the following who contributed material to this book:

J. W. Hall; A. K. Austin; W. H. Irvin; T. P. Adderson; Mrs. Bridger; Leslie Todd; Rev. A. Daemond Hall; Mrs. E. W. Tritton; D. Mackie; C. K. Langstaff; J. D. Rhodes; Mrs. L. E. Rogers; Mrs. C. Gregory; Rev. N. Walker; Mrs. P. J. Hunt; W. M. Paton; Mrs. B. Gage; Miss M. Burgess; W. Warcup; A. J. Cornwell; J. Whitcombe; J. Pearson; B. G. Ellis; A. M. Thomson; Miss K. Diegan; G. S. F. Hicks; J. Dunford; A. G. Handel; Mrs T. Smith; G. A. Hartley; J. Fleming; J. A. Coxall; Miss C. A. Burton; A. Mac L. Currie; I. Ryan; M. Ryan; Miss K. Greville; Rev. J. Christie; Mrs. P. A. Edwards; Mrs. L. G. Beavers; M. Hawkins; Mrs. C. H. Jones; J. Dolan; S. J. Sanders; Mrs. B. E. Johnson; Sister M. Emilia; R. J. Owen; Miss J. Meyrick; Mrs. E. Battersby; M. Taylor; L. Mizzi; E. C. Fleming; M. Johns; F. Else; B. G. Ellis; M. S. Howard; J. Whitcombe; D. J. Charlick; W. W. Rogers; Mrs. D. M. Castell; Catriona; Sara Cole; Mrs. E. Nelson; Mrs. P. Parkinson; G. Wraight; D. Harris; G. Cullerford; A. Barclay; W. B. N. Oates; C. Harold; Mrs. S. Elsey; Rev. C. Clarkowski; M. E. Tester; M. Hawkins; Miss P. J. Hunt; J. Dunford; N. Pearson; M. Cassidy; A. J. Cornwell; Mrs. M. V. Medd; J. W. Hall; T. P. Adderson; A. E. Bissell; C. K. Lanstaff; H. S. Craig; Mrs. M. George; G. Watson.

And to A. R. Mowbray and Co. Ltd. for permission to use the four poems from *Saints and Sinods* by S. J. Forrest